A sister is love mixed with friendship and with a million favorite memories that will always last.

— Carey Martin

Blue Mountain Arts®

New and Best-Selling Titles

Daring to Be Ourselves
from Interviews by Marianne Schnall

A Daughter Is Life's Greatest Gift

For You, Just Because You're Very Special to Me
by Douglas Pagels

For You, My Soul Mate
by Douglas Pagels

Friends Are Forever
by Marci

A Girl's Guide to College
by Traci Maynigo

God Is Always Watching Over You

I Thanked God for You Today
by Donna Fargo

Keep Believing in Yourself and Your Dreams

The Love Between a Mother and Daughter Is Forever

The Path to Success Is Paved with Positive Thinking
by Wally Amos with Stu Glauberman

Required Reading for All Teenagers
Written and Edited by Douglas Pagels

A Sister's Love Is Forever

A Son Is Life's Greatest Gift

The Strength of Women

Take Time for You
by M. Butler and D. Mastromarino

Think Positive Thoughts Every Day

To My Daughter with Love on the Important Things in Life
by Susan Polis Schutz

To My One True Love
by Susan Polis Schutz

To My Son with Love
by Susan Polis Schutz

Today, I Will...
by James Downton, Jr.

A
Sister's
Love
Is Forever

A Very Special Collection
to Share with a Sister
Who Is More Than Family...
She's a Friend for Life

Edited by Angela Joshi

Blue Mountain Press™
Boulder, Colorado

We wish to thank Susan Polis Schutz for permission to reprint the following poem that appears in this publication: "Dreams can come true...." Copyright © 1988 by Stephen Schutz and Susan Polis Schutz. All rights reserved.

Library of Congress Control Number: 2011907084
ISBN: 978-1-59842-622-9

◾ and Blue Mountain Press are registered in U.S. Patent and Trademark Office.
Certain trademarks are used under license.

Printed in China.
First Printing: 2011

♻ This book is printed on recycled paper.

This book is printed on paper that has been specially produced to be acid free (neutral pH) and contains no groundwood or unbleached pulp. It conforms with the requirements of the American National Standards Institute, Inc., so as to ensure that this book will last and be enjoyed by future generations.

Blue Mountain Arts, Inc.
P.O. Box 4549, Boulder, Colorado 80306

Contents

I'm Glad You're
My Sister

Have I ever told you
how glad I am
that you're my sister?
I'm telling you now
because I want you to know
how very important you are to me
and just how much love
there is for you
deep within my heart.

Too often, Sister,
the beautiful things in life
are taken for granted,
and I realize that you
are one of the most beautiful
aspects of mine.
That's why it's so important
for me to tell you now
that you are special to me.
You're more than just family;
you are a friend,
a confidante,
and a shoulder to lean on
in times of need.

You're the person I always
want to share everything with —
each dream, each goal I attain,
each sorrow, each joy.
If I have never told you before
how glad I am
that you're my sister,
I'm telling you now.
I want you to know
that you mean the world to me,
and I will love you
with all my heart… forever.

— Deanne Laura Pool

There Are Three Things I'll Always Try to Do for You, Sister

There's nobody like you, and there never will be — not in my life, at least. You are a world apart from everyone else. No one can ever take your place with me. You've got your own special corner of my heart all to yourself.

And because you mean so much to me, there are three things I'm going to make sure I try to do as often as I can...

I am going to remind you for years and years to come how wonderful and unique you really are (just in case you forget it sometimes!).

I'm going to do what I can to be there for you… and hope that in some small way I can pay back a tiny bit of all the happiness you've given me.

And I'm going to say "thanks" every chance I get. Thanks from my heart, thanks from my smiles, and thank you immensely… for just being you!

— Kelly Lise

More Than Sisters

What are the infinite chances that of
all the zillions of people in the world,
God would see fit to make
    the two of us sisters?

The common bond between us
goes far beyond mere bloodlines.
We find joy in each other's triumphs
and sorrow in each other's pain.
We share a sibling intimacy that
    defies description...
a family connection that
    forever binds us to one another.

But the greatest miracle of all
is a blessing I will never take lightly.
Beyond the connections, the bloodlines,
and all the family ties,
we are so much more than sisters.
Between us is a relationship
more rare and precious
    than any worldly treasure...
for we are also friends.

— Suzy Toronto

As family, sisters share
a very secure closeness.
But when friendship emerges
    from their closeness,
something even more special happens...
A strong bond develops that
    brings them even closer to each other.
The bond is so powerful that
    it not only brings them added joy...
it also comforts and befriends
    each sister with loyalty,
compassion, and understanding
that cannot be measured.
Regardless of differences,
    miles between them,
or anything that can separate them,
sisters who become friends are
always a part of each other.
They are the answer to each other's
    spoken and unspoken needs
and a gift of love to each other's heart.

— Susan Hickman Sater

If I were to write down all the things that are so wonderful about having you for a sister, the list would be long enough to reach all the way from my door to yours… and back again.

I can't imagine why I was so beautifully blessed to have been given the gift of a sister like you, but I'm sure glad I was. Our special connection means more to me with the passing of every year. We have a friendship that just keeps blossoming… and a love we can count on to never go away.

There are times when my eyes fill up with tears just from thinking of how dear you are. But there are many more times when my heart fills up with smiles just from knowing how close and caring we'll always be.

You're really something. And you're so loved, so treasured, and so enormously appreciated by me.

— Sandy Jamison

14

The Love Between
Us Is Forever

The love between us is a bond that can never be broken. There may be fights and disagreements, but they never last long. There may be tears, but they will always be washed away by laughter. We have a silent understanding deep within our hearts — an unspoken promise to always be there for each other no matter what, sharing secrets, hugs, and heart-to-heart talks.

The love between us is made up of more than family ties. It is the best kind of friendship — the kind that knows every memory and every bit of history, as well as every hope and dream for tomorrow. It is a constant, warm reminder that there will always be someone who understands, who cares, who supports and loves with the most unconditional kind of love in the world.

— Carol Thomas

As Sisters, We Share Something Special

Through the years,
we've gone through many
good and bad times together.
There have been things
    that we've disagreed on
and things that have brought us
    so close together.
There have been the silences
    that sisters, no matter how close,
        must hear,
and there has been the laughter
    that only sisters share.
But through the years,
    I've always known that
no one could ever replace you
    and the love we share.

— Ann Rudacille

Who else would I rather turn to
when I have a big piece of news
or when I am just looking to chat?
We know each other inside and out.
We understand each other's
hardships and triumphs,
dreams and goals,
friendships and love life,
and likes and dislikes.

It's nice to be at that place
in a relationship where we can
get right to the heart of the matter.
I don't have to worry about
being misunderstood or judged.
I know your love is the lasting kind.

It's not hard to see we're
very lucky to have each other.
We've got every reason to celebrate
our special connection as sisters.

— Rebecca Brown

No one can take the place of a sister.
No one makes you feel as safe and welcome
or as understood, accepted, and embraced.

No one can take the place of a sister —
in private jokes that are lost
on anyone but the two of you;
in lighthearted exchanges
that define your connection;
in the encouragement
she effortlessly provides
to your spirit and your heart;
in the advice she so gently lends;
in the support you know is always yours;
and in the forever friend you have in her.

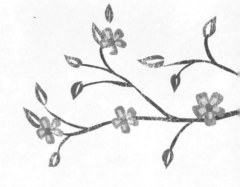

Sister, please know
I cherish the gift of our connection
every single day.
I am forever grateful for
your irreplaceable presence in my life.

— Lynn Keachie

My Sister Is...

My sister is my heart.
She opens doors to rooms
I never knew were there,
breaks through walls
I don't recall building.
She lights my darkest corners
with the sparkle in her eyes.

My sister is my soul.
She inspires my wearied spirit
to fly on wings of angels.
But while I hold her hand,
my feet never leave the ground.
She stills my deepest fears
with the wisdom of her song.

My sister is my past.
She writes my history.
In her eyes I recognize myself —
memories only we can share.
She remembers, she forgives,
and she accepts me as I am
with tender understanding.

My sister is my future.
She lives within my dreams.
She sees my undiscovered secrets
and believes in me as I stumble.
She walks in step with me,
her love lighting my way.

My sister is my strength.
She hears the whispered prayers
that I cannot speak.
She helps me find my smile,
freely giving hers away.
She catches my tears
in her gentle hands.

My sister is like no one else.
She's my most treasured friend,
filling up the empty spaces
and healing broken places.
She is my rock, my inspiration.
Though impossible to define,
in a word, she is... my sister.

— Lisa Lorden

We've shared secret dreams
and childhood pranks.
Together, we slipped into
the kitchen for midnight snacks,
wheedled each other
for the latest tales,
and whispered our private hopes
into each other's ears.

You've always been there
by my side,
offering me a secure place
in your heart.
I know you always love me
and I can turn to you anytime.
I am so thankful
you are my sister and friend.
You are the corner piece
to my puzzle.
You complete me.
You are my sparkle in life.

— Terri Tiffany

Little Sister

You have grown in the blink of an eye. You have turned into a strong woman: confident, radiant, and independent.

You carry yourself with strength and assurance, taking one certain step after another into the busy world. Although you may stumble, you will not fall. Your light heart helps you see humor in the world and yourself. Your passion drives you to fight injustice, and your soul celebrates the beauty of the world.

I stand on the sidelines of your life —
mourning your disappointments, feeling your
heartbreaks, celebrating your successes,
and swelling with pride that you are my
little sister.

I am excited to see your life continue to
unfold. You have the future in your hands.
You will make a huge difference, whatever
road you choose.

— Tabatha Goodwin

Shared Memories

You keep your past by having sisters. As you get older, they're the only ones who don't get bored if you talk about your memories.

— Deborah Moggach

I find it comforting to have a sister who can remember all the mundane and dramatic things that happened around us as children. I always find it uniquely reassuring to discuss childhood memories with my sister. She's my connection to my past, the only person who can help me remember what happened.

— Marcia Millman

Sisters are memories of pillow fights, whispered secrets, ice-cream cones, and castles hidden in the clouds. Sisters are memories of running through the sprinklers on a hot summer day, wishing on dandelions, making cookies and licking the spatula clean. Sisters are memories of all the best things in life.

— Rachyl Taylor

Big Sister

I've known you all my life. You were always right there with me — guiding me, advising me, coaching me. You encouraged me, taught me, and at times scolded me. You tried to protect and shield me from the trials and tribulations of growing up. When you realized you couldn't, you helped me through them. At the time, I didn't appreciate all your effort. Now that we're all grown up, I understand how lucky I was to have a big sister like you.

— Colleen Tillger

When we were younger, I thought you were the absolute coolest thing on two legs! I wanted to dress like you, walk like you, talk like you, and have as many friends as you did.

I realize now that you weren't just a wonderful sister — you were a wonderful friend, too. You listened to what I had to say, no matter how silly, and you helped me learn so many things only a big sister knows.

We're hardly kids anymore, but I still think you are one amazing sister and one amazing woman. I can't even imagine not having you as my sister.

— Rachel Snyder

The Bond of Childhood

No one knows better than a sister how we grew up, and who our friends, teachers, and favorite toys were. No one knows better than she the inner workings of our family, our parents' private and public selves. Although as an adult you and your sister may live in very different worlds... you are sharing a strong bond: the source from which you've learned about life.

— Dale V. Atkins

It occurs to me that one can never grow up with one's sister. In some secret place we remain seven and eight. And yet we are always family, tied by bonds so deep, so invisible.

— Patricia Foster

A sister is a little bit of childhood that can never be lost.

— Marion Garretty

You Are My Truest Friend

No matter how many
wonderful friends
we each have in our lives,
there's no one on earth
who knows me the way you do.
We share a past, present, and future
that only those linked by the love of family
can ever fully inhabit.
When I think about your understanding
of who I am — and who I'm not —
I realize no friend could ever be
closer to me than you.

Together, we have celebrated
so many birthdays
and special family days,
and they've all made memories
that last and last.
I love thinking back on
the fun and the laughter —
and even the fights and forgiveness —
because they all played such a big role
in this great sister friendship
we get to share forever.

— Elizabeth Rose

Now that we are older
and so many things in our lives
    have changed,
I realize how lucky we are
to have shared so many
    wonderful times.

Being children together was easy;
becoming adults was a challenge.
Yet now I think of you
and feel so proud for you
and the accomplishments you have
    made in your life.
I know you are special to others,
and you are always special to me.

You are my sister,
and with all my heart,
I hope that all your dreams
for tomorrow will come true
and that love
will be with you forever.

— Deanna Beisser

What a Remarkable Person You Are

There are so many times
when I am in awe of you.

And I want you to know
that I admire you so much!

I admire
the life that you lead and the
kindness that is such a sweet and
natural part of you.

I admire
the way you treat other people.

I admire
how easily a smile finds its way
to your face.

I admire
the work that you do and the
places your journeys take you.

I admire
your dedication to all the right
things and your devotion to your
friends and your family.

I admire
how completely you care and how
willingly you are always there
for the people who need you.

I admire
so many things about you, and I
thank you with all my heart for
being the light that you are...
to my life.

— L. N. Mallory

You are such an important
person in my life —
one of the few people
who care so much
and expect so little in return.
I have always felt like
I can count on you for anything
and that I would never be let down.

You go out of your way
to make my life happier,
and the little things you do
mean so very much to me.
You have such a big heart
filled with so much kindness
    and love.
I feel so very lucky to know you
and so very blessed to have you
    in my life.
                    — Elle Mastro

You are the most beautiful person I know —
not just outside, but inside, too.
You have a wonderful sense of humor,
a loyalty that not many people have,
and the gift of love you give to others.

We may not be perfect;
we have our share of arguments,
our times of laughter,
and our share of troubles.
Yet we can always trust
each other with anything.

When you just have to share something,
good or bad, I will listen.
You are the world to me.
Words can't express my appreciation,
but it means a lot to me
that you are my sister,
and I will love you forever.
A sister like you
is the greatest gift in the world.

— Kristy Jorgensen

Sisters are united
by a heritage of love and laughter,
dreams and memories
of growing up together,
and shared stories of journeys into adulthood.

As little girls we dreamed of growing up
and doing something wonderful;
as adults we found it wasn't as easy
as we'd hoped.
I'm here to remind you to stay connected
to your deepest dreams.
Your girlhood still holds a secret key
to becoming the woman
you always wanted to be.

Trust that little girl inside.
Let her remind you
of what is most important in life.
Draw from her idealism so you may see
the world with the purity of a child's eyes.

Know you are capable and lovable,
dare to dream,
and find your heart's desire.
And when you look in the mirror,
remember the sister who loves you
and believes in you.

— Candy Paull

You Are a Beautiful, Courageous, Outstanding Woman

Believe in yourself
as I believe in you.
Trust in your strengths
as I trust in them.

Look in the mirror
and see what I see —
a talented, uplifting,
and magnificent woman
who can do anything
and everything she wants.

Believe in your heart
that you have the power
to grab hold of your future
and mold it into the things
you have always dreamed of.

Trust in your soul
that you are capable of doing
all that needs to be done.

Know that you are
incredible in every way,
and see yourself
as others see you…
as an intelligent
and spectacular woman.

— Lamisha Serf

Dreams can come true
if you take the time to
think about what you want in life
Get to know yourself
Find out who you are
Choose your goals carefully
Be honest with yourself
Always believe in yourself
Find many interests and pursue them
Find out what is important to you
Find out what you are good at
Don't be afraid to make mistakes
Work hard to achieve successes
When things are not going right
don't give up — just try harder
Find courage inside of you to remain strong
Give yourself freedom to try out new things
Don't be so set in your ways that you can't grow
Always act in an ethical way

Laugh and have a good time
Form relationships with people you respect
Treat others as you want them to treat you
Be honest with people
Accept the truth
Speak the truth
Open yourself up to love
Don't be afraid to love
Remain close to your family
Take part in the beauty of nature
Be appreciative of all that you have
Help those less fortunate than you
Try to make other lives happy
Work toward peace in the world
Live life to the fullest
Create your own dreams
and your dreams will become a reality

— Susan Polis Schutz

When I Look
at You, Sister...

I see a remarkable woman
with a kind and caring heart
who is beautiful in every sense of the word
I see a smile that lights up the room
and laughter that is truly contagious
I see strength and wisdom
beyond anything I have ever known
I see love — pure and true
compassion and thoughtfulness
I see a woman who walks
through this world with gentleness and grace

I admire you for all that you are
and for all that you do
You are everything wonderful in this world
and if I had just one wish it would be
that you could see what I see when I look at you

— Elle Mastro

You are such a beautiful part of my life. And although you don't get to hear my thanks nearly often enough, there are so many times when it feels like my heart is overflowing with an amazing amount of appreciation for you.

I wish I could thank you endlessly… for all the smiles, all the support, all the hugs and the love and the wisdom. Thank you for caring so much.

I want you to know this today and I hope you'll remember it always: I feel like I've been blessed with someone who brings me more happiness and peace of mind… than most people even dream of. That someone is you.

— Marta Best

Warm-hearted people always seem to find a way to make others feel good. They do not look for rewards or medals. They do good things just because they care. They add a spark of joy to the lives they touch and leave a lasting impression on us forever.

Thank you for being one of those wonderful, caring people… and for touching my heart with your kindness.
— Debra Heintz Cavataio

The Story of Two Very Different Sisters

One is here; one lives there. One is a little taller than the other. They have two different colors of hair, two different outlooks on life, two very different views from their windows. Both have different tomorrows ahead. Each is unique in so many ways. Each has her own story, with all the busy things going on in the present. Each has different work to do and different demands on the day. Each has a separate destination and a distinctly different path to get there. But...

For all the things that might be different
and unique about them… these two
sisters will always share so much. They will
always be the best of family <u>and</u> friends,
entwined together, through all the days
of their lives. Their love will always be very
special: gentle and joyful when it can be,
strong and giving when it needs to be,
reminding them, no matter how different
their stories turn out, they share the
incredibly precious gift of being "sisters."
And when you think of some of the best
things this world has to offer, a blessing
like that is really what it's all about.

— Laurel Atherton

The Miracle of Sisterhood

We're not always best friends.
We're very different.
We still give each other
    unsolicited advice
and even fight sometimes.
We get too busy to visit;
    we often drift away.
But we always come back…
because we're sisters.

The miracle of sisterhood
is that whatever separates us
has less power over us
than the memories,
experiences, and feelings
of being family.
And these ties welcome us
home to each other's heart.

We are never so separated
    by arguments
that we can't reunite in compromise.
We praise each other's strengths
and use them for our mutual benefit.
Our busy schedules still include
time for nurturing each other.
The child in each of us still
remembers all the fun times
we had growing up.
Despite our differences,
we come together
to recapture that happiness
and make it part of our
    lives today...
because we are sisters.

— Jacqueline Schiff

We Will Always Be Sisters First

I know there are times when we don't see things the same way. We may disagree with each other's ideas or the choices we make. But I also know that the love we have deep down will always be there.

At times, it might take us a while to figure out how to reconnect or learn to appreciate each other for the women we have become. But I believe we can always find a way.

— Christa Winters

Even though the back-seat battles are in the past, our relationship is still tested occasionally by a disagreement or crisis. But we have been strengthened — as individuals and as sisters — by what we have learned from our childhood experiences.

— Dale V. Atkins

A Sister's Love Is a Wonderful Love to Have

I depend so much on having your love in my life. Whether we are discussing every detail of our lives over the phone or we haven't seen each other in what seems like forever, I know that you are always there and our hearts will never lose touch.

You give me a sense of security: a feeling that no matter what mistakes I make or where life takes me, you will always accept me — and like me — for who I am.

I know that even if we fight, the caring and respect we have for each other will never be damaged or destroyed.

Our relationship makes me feel rooted and connected. We belong to one another — in the past, present, and future — and nothing can weaken that bond. Other loves may come and go, but ours is guaranteed for a lifetime.

— Pamela Koehlinger

A sister is someone more
special than words can even begin
   to describe.

She is love mixed with friendship
and with a million favorite memories that
   will always last.

A sister is a hand within yours,
enfolded with hope
and understanding.
She is a warm-hearted soul
who always knows the innermost things —
your secrets and worries and wishes
and dreams — when no one else
   even comes close.

And every day of your life,
she gives you a feeling
that makes you wonder
what you would
   ever do without her...

Because no one
is loved so dearly,
and no one is
   appreciated so much.
                    — Carey Martin

There's Nothing like a Sister

You know full as well as I do the value of sisters' affection to each other; there is nothing like it in this earth.

— Charlotte Brontë

A sister is a confidante.
A sister is a friend.
A sister is there
when no one else
could understand.
A sister is a miracle.
A sister is a dream come true.
A sister is a friend for life.

— Ashley Rice

A sister protects you from all harm
and is always near when you need her.
She's a friend who listens forever
when others turn away.
She brings sunshine where
there are clouds;
she is like a breath of spring
through the storms of winter,
a guiding star in the darkness of night.
She smiles at you when others frown
and welcomes you with open arms.
She accepts you for who you are
and doesn't expect you to be
anyone else.
She thinks that you're the best,
and makes you feel so important
that you start to believe it yourself.
There's no one like a sister.

— Geri Danks

How to Be
the Best Sister
in the World

Start by just being yourself… because the person you are is so wonderful! ✦ Then… be all the amazing things you've always been to me: a helper, a guide, a confidante, a friend. ✦ Know that it's okay to throw in a little bit of teasing along with all the caring in your heart. ✦ Realize that our family ties are so strong when they need to be, our laughter is so sweet when it wants to be, and our bond is always going to be there, no matter what. ✦

Know that we've grown up... but we'll never outgrow a wish to stay as close as possible. ✦ Remember... no matter how high the walls may be between other people, there is an open door between us that always leads to love. ✦

And keep on being the kind of sister who makes me happy in ways that there will never be enough words for. ✦ When the words come from my heart, I know you always listen with yours. ✦ And one of the things I hope you'll never forget... is how thankful I am for you. ✦ When it comes to being a sister, I've got five special words to say to you: you really are the best!

— Sandy Jamison

You Are My Guardian Angel

You touch my life
in a million ways.
You make me proud
for so many reasons.
You are the sister
anyone would love to have!

Sometimes I think you are
a guardian angel in disguise.
You've always looked out for me
and treated me as a friend.

We know each other so well.
Sometimes we don't even need words.
It's as if you can read what is
on my mind and in my heart.
And so often I can tell
by the expression on your face
or the tone of your voice
where you're coming from, too.
I believe that's what makes
our relationship so special and lasting.

True sisters are two people
who understand each other,
respect each other,
look out for each other,
and love each other unconditionally…
and you're as true as they get!

— Dianne Cogar

Best Friends
for Life

I'm so thankful that
I will always have you in my life
to understand me, love me,
accept me, and reaffirm me.
No one else could ever fill your place,
not in a million years.

You are such a bright light
to so many people.
You inspire me in so many ways.
You've touched my heart
and changed my life,
just by being your amazing,
wonderful self.
I hope you never, ever forget
how precious you are.

The greatest blessing I ever received
was having you for a sister.
You're an integral part of my life.
My love for you is steady and constant,
just like the beat of my own heart.
I'll be here with you always,
for each and every bend in the road.
I'll be here cheering for you,
encouraging you,
and giving thanks for you every day.
We're best friends for life.

— Rebecca Brown

You Will Always Be a Part of Me

There is never a time in my life
when I'm not with you in some way.
There are moments
when you come to mind more strongly,
sometimes in a special way,
but you are with me always.
Sometimes you are with me
in the warm memory
of some laughter we've shared.
I admire your personality,
your character,
and the qualities you possess.
You are a capable and
determined person.

There is an understanding
we have developed,
a relationship that shows we care,
and a oneness that has grown
out of respect, patience, and love.
If I could give you
the happiness and success
that you *deserve,*
it would last forever.
I wish you all that you *desire*
and all that is beautiful.
You will forever be a part
of me and my life.

— Victor Barbella

My Sister's Heart

Sister, your heart has been the one
I've trusted with my deepest truths —
knowing they'd remain both
guarded and understood.

Your heart has been attentive
to all that matters most to me —
listening to me in comfort
    and support.

Your heart has kept me smiling
through all the ages and stages
we've passed through —
and it has loved me
without question or fail
all the blessed days of my life.

I thank you with love and gratitude
for the countless gifts
of your heart —
trusting in return
that you will always find
a home in my heart, too.

— Lynn Keachie

We Are Family

The best feeling in this world
    is family.
From it, we draw love,
    friendship, moral support,
and the fulfillment of every
    special need within our hearts.

In a family, we are connected to
    an ever-present source
of sunny moments, smiles and laughter,
understanding and encouragement,
and hugs that help us grow
    in confidence all along life's path.

Wherever we are,
whatever we're doing,
whenever we really need to feel
especially loved, befriended,
supported, and cared for
in the greatest way,
our hearts can turn to family
and find the very best
always waiting for us.

— Barbara J. Hall

There's No Place like Home

We've been each other's instructors in the classroom of life. We've taught each other how to show love and how not to. We've influenced each other's destiny because of our common bond, and we all know how good it feels to have a family.

Together, we've learned the importance of loyalty and discipline, acceptance and encouragement, attitude and character. We've pouted and thrown tantrums; we've been sweet and thoughtful and stubborn.

We've supported and defended each other; we've been hopeful and disappointed together. Through it all, you have taught me about the need for understanding and the significance of knowing that some things in life won't change — like family. I know we may have felt a little dysfunctional at times, but I am thankful that we're in our family together and that we have a lot of good memories to share. Because of you, there's no place like home.

— Donna Fargo

I'm Always Here for You

I know you don't always have the time
to sit and have a cup of coffee with me
or to give me a call every day.
I realize that life's demands on you
are more than you feel
you can handle at times.
I know you sometimes wonder
how you will get through each day.
But take a look —
I am still here for you.
You may think I won't understand;
but don't worry,
I am not here to judge you.

We may drift apart from time to time,
but we are bound together in spirit.
So when your burdens get too heavy
or you feel as though you need
some appreciation,
know that I will be here for you...
always.

— Elizabeth Luera

In your happiest and most exciting moments, my heart will celebrate and smile beside you. In your lowest lows, my love will be there to keep you warm, to give you strength, and to remind you that your sunshine is sure to come again.

In your moments of accomplishment, I will be filled so full of pride that I may have a hard time keeping the feeling inside me.

In your moments of disappointment, I will be a shoulder to cry on, a hand to hold, and a love that will gently enfold you until everything's okay. In your gray days, I will help you search, one by one, for the colors of the rainbow.

— Alin Austin

I Am So Grateful
for You, Sister

The weather changes. The world changes. People and times change, as well. But the one thing that remains forever constant in my life is you, my sister.

How can I ever thank you for being all that you are to me? All my life I have always had you to count on… and even now, with our lives constantly moving in different directions, I still feel the same comfort I've always had just knowing that you are in the world.

We may not be able to spend every day together the way we used to, but you are still the person I love to laugh with and the person I turn to when life's got me down. I want you to know that our lives may change and we may find ourselves changing, too, but we will always be family, and I will always be grateful that I have you in my life.

— Elle Mastro

Sisters Are Forever

To have a loving relationship with a sister is not simply to have a buddy or a confidante — it is to have a soul mate for life.

— Victoria Secunda

Each morning when the day begins,
when other friendships fade or end...
sisters are forever.

Seasons come and seasons go.
Summer rains turn into snow.

But no matter where you live
or how far you go...

sisters are forever.

— Ashley Rice

Thank You

There are a few things you truly deserve to know and some precious thoughts I'd love for you to hold on to forever. Most of all, I want to tell you this…

Thank you for being such a good soul. You have been a huge inspiration to me, and you have had a very special influence on my life.

Thank you for being someone I can trust with the key to everything about me. I love that I can tell you anything and that I can turn to you at any hour of the day or night.

Thank you for the endless hours of joy. Thank you for drying any tears.

Thank you for helping me stay strong when my own strength isn't quite enough.

And thank you... sweetly and immensely... for the way you touch my life and share so many moments of this journey.

I really want you to remember that you are incredibly treasured by me.

And you always will be.

— Chris Gallatin

When I look back
through the years
and think of all
you've done for me,
I am overwhelmed
with a sense of gratitude.

Quite simply,
there are not enough words
in the English language
that could repay you
for all you have done for me.
You have cared for me, stood by me,
and loved me in countless ways.
You have played an irreplaceable role
in my growth from child to adult.
I love you. I thank you.
May you be blessed in all the ways
you have blessed me.

— Silvia Demaras

Sisters Carry Each Other
in Their Hearts
Forever and Always

Whether they live near each other or far apart, sisters walk through life together. They're there for each other no matter what... sharing everything.

Sisters are connected at the heart and in their blood, and their loyalty to one another is permanent. No one can ever break that bond. They don't give up on each other easily. They have the utmost sensitivity and compassion for one another because they were born into the same family.

Sisters aren't afraid to break rules for each other. They defend each other; they take chances for each other. They've cried together and laughed together. They know each other's secrets. They forgive each other when they make mistakes, and they can almost read each other's mind.

Sisters teach each other lessons as they stand by each other in life, and they are there for each other through everything that matters.

No one can ever take the place of a sister. Thank you for being mine.

— Donna Fargo

Wishes for a Wonderful Sister

You are such a wonderful sister, and you are so deserving of every good thing and every brighter day that could ever be wished.

I hope all the things you long for will find their way into your life.

May the days be good to you: comforting more often than crazy and giving more often than taking.

May the passing seasons make sure that any heartaches are replaced with a million smiles and that any hard journeys eventually turn into nice, easy miles that take you everywhere you want to go.

May your dreams do their absolute best to come true.

May your heart be filled with the kindness
   of friends, the caring of everyone you
   love, and the richness of memories you
   wouldn't trade for anything.
May life's little worries always stay small.
May you get a little closer every day to
   any goals you want to achieve.
May any changes be good ones and any
   challenges turn out to be for the better.
May you find time to do the things you've
   always wanted to do!

And may you be happy... forever.

— Douglas Pagels

Acknowledgments

We gratefully acknowledge the permission granted by the following authors, publishers, and authors' representatives to reprint poems or excerpts from their publications: Suzy Toronto for "More Than Sisters." Copyright © 2008 by Suzy Toronto. All rights reserved. Lynn Keachie for "No one can take the place of a sister." Copyright © 2011 by Lynn Keachie. All rights reserved. Terri Tiffany for "We've shared secret dreams...." Copyright © 2011 by Terri Tiffany. All rights reserved. Tabatha Goodwin for "Little Sister." Copyright © 2011 by Tabatha Goodwin. All rights reserved. HarperCollins Publishers for "You keep your past by having..." by Deborah Moggach from SISTER SETS by Emily Gwathmey and Ellen Stern. Copyright © 1996 by Emily Gwathmey and Ellen Stern. All rights reserved. Houghton Mifflin Harcourt Publishing Company for "I find it comforting to..." from THE PERFECT SISTER by Marcia Millman. Copyright © 2004 by Marcia Millman. Reprinted by permission. All rights reserved. Rachel Snyder for "When we were younger...." Copyright © 2011 by Rachel Snyder. All rights reserved. Dr. Dale Atkins for "No one knows better than a sister..." and "Even though the back-seat battles..." from SISTERS. Copyright © 1984 by Dale V. Atkins. All rights reserved. Patricia Foster for "It occurs to me that one..." from SISTER TO SISTER. Copyright © 1995 by Patricia Foster. All rights reserved. Kelly Pullen for "What It Means to Have a Sister." Copyright © 2011 by Kelly Pullen. All rights reserved. Candy Paull for "Sisters are united by a heritage...." Copyright © 2011 by Candy Paull. All rights reserved. Lamisha Serf for "You Are a Beautiful, Courageous, Outstanding Woman." Copyright © 2011 by Lamisha Serf. All rights reserved. Jacqueline Schiff for "The Miracle of Sisterhood." Copyright © 2011 by Jacqueline Schiff. All rights reserved. Christa Winters for "We Will Always Be Sisters First." Copyright © 2011 by Christa Winters. All rights reserved. Dianne Cogar for "You Are My Guardian Angel." Copyright © 2011 by Dianne Cogar. All rights reserved. PrimaDonna Entertainment Corp. for "There's No Place like Home" and "Sisters Carry Each Other in Their Hearts Forever and Always" by Donna Fargo. Copyright © 2002, 2011 by PrimaDonna Entertainment Corp. All rights reserved. Elizabeth Luera for "I'm Always Here for You." Copyright © 2011 by Elizabeth Luera. All rights reserved. Victoria Secunda for "To have a loving relationship...." Copyright © 1998 by Victoria Secunda. All rights reserved. Silvia Demaras for "When I look back through the years...." Copyright © 2011 by Silvia Demaras. All rights reserved.

A careful effort has been made to trace the ownership of selections used in this anthology in order to obtain permission to reprint copyrighted material and give proper credit to the copyright owners. If any error or omission has occurred, it is completely inadvertent, and we would like to make corrections in future editions provided that written notification is made to the publisher:

BLUE MOUNTAIN ARTS, INC., P.O. Box 4549, Boulder, Colorado 80306.